Big Jag Looks for Fish

By Sally Cowan

Big Jag did not have milk for her cub, Tot.

Sit in the den, Tot! I will get a fish.

Big Jag hid in some rocks
and looked for fish.

Big Jag can see a big fin!

She rushed off the rocks
to get it!

Whack!

Big Jag splashed
and splashed.

But the fish was too quick!

Big Jag went back
and hid in the rocks.

She had a big moth
for a snack,
but it was not much.

Then, Big Jag got up,
as quick as a whip!

She rushed to get a fish.

Whack!

Big Jag got back to her den with the fish in her fangs.

Tot had a sniff of the fish and then a lick!

Big Jag and Tot mashed up the big fish.

Yum, yum!

CHECKING FOR MEANING

1. Why did Big Jag hide in the rocks? *(Literal)*

2. Why did Big Jag eat a moth? *(Literal)*

3. Did Tot enjoy eating the fish? How do you know? *(Inferential)*

EXTENDING VOCABULARY

Whack	What is the meaning of *Whack*? What other words have the same meaning? Can you remember what we call words that imitate the sound made by the person or object in the book? i.e. onomatopoeia.
much	The word *much* refers to an amount. Can you use it in other sentences to show its meanings? e.g. *I didn't have much to eat. I didn't get much sleep last night. How much money do I need?*
lick	What part of your body do you use to *lick* something? Why do we lick things? What do you sometimes lick? Do animals lick? What do they lick?

MOVING BEYOND THE TEXT

1. Why did Big Jag have to catch a fish to share with Tot?

2. What is a snack? What snacks do you eat? When do you eat them?

3. Why do we sometimes smell foods we haven't eaten before?

4. What other foods do jaguars eat in the wild? How do they catch it?

SPEED SOUNDS

| sh | ch | th | th | ck | ng |

voiced   unvoiced

PRACTICE WORDS

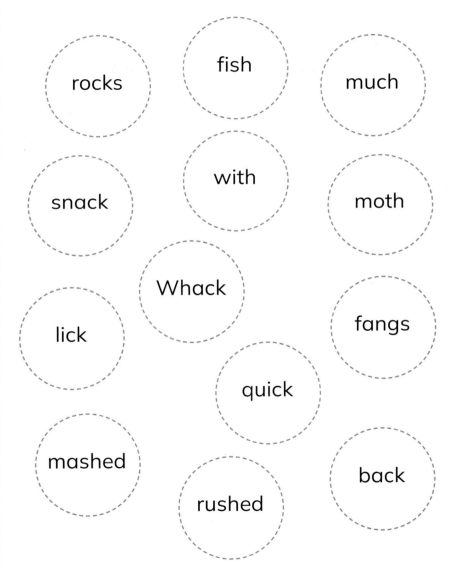

rocks

fish

much

snack

with

moth

Whack

lick

fangs

quick

mashed

back

rushed